100+ SARCASTIC HR-AUTHORIZED

WAYS TO TELL
COWORKERS THEY'RE

STUPID

"Have you checked my last email?"

"Seriously, stop sending me emails every minute."

"To ensure effective communication, please combine all daily updates into one email"

PAUL DEV

Disclaimer

This book is solely for entertainment purposes
and contains occasional mild profanity, so it
may not be suitable for all audiences. And no
certified HR professional has approved these
answers, so use them as you see fit.

What I Really Want To Say Out Loud

Get a life.

What I'd Say To Avoid Getting Fired

I suggest you to focus on your own priorities and interests.

What I Really Want To Say Out Loud

Use common sense.

What I'd Say To Avoid Getting Fired

Maybe we could rethink this and approach it differently.

What I Really Want To Say Out Loud

Keep your opinion to yourself. I don't need it, nor will I use it.

What I'd Say To Avoid Getting Fired

Your opinion is noted and will be given the attention it deserves. (Just none!)

What I Really Want To Say Out Loud

Punctuality isn't in your dictionary.

What I'd Say To Avoid Getting Fired

Arriving on time ensures efficient meetings and workflow.

What I Really Want To Say Out Loud

Stealing my work? Real classy.

What I'd Say To Avoid Getting Fired

I am happy to see my ideas reaching a wider audience. Could you please confirm when and how I will be credited?

What I Really Want To Say Out Loud

You're so full of yourself.

What I'd Say To Avoid Getting Fired

This is a team effort, so everyone's input is valuable.

What I Really Want To Say Out Loud

You're stupid.

What I'd Say To Avoid Getting Fired

I'm afraid it seems there's been a misunderstanding here. Let's clear things up.

What I Really Want To Say Out Loud

Sure, my favorite thing is doing your job for you.

What I'd Say To Avoid Getting Fired

While I can assist this time, we should plan better for future projects.

What I Really Want To Say Out Loud

You're a pain in the ass.

What I'd Say To Avoid Getting Fired

I have observed that some of your actions have occasionally been distracting.

What I Really Want To Say Out Loud

Late again and expecting us to cover it. Typical.

What I'd Say To Avoid Getting Fired

Being on time is essential for a positive and productive start.

What I Really Want To Say Out Loud

You're f*cking lying, you a*shole.

What I'd Say To Avoid Getting Fired

Actually, I remember that a bit differently.

What I Really Want To Say Out Loud

Lazy as hell. Get to work.

What I'd Say To Avoid Getting Fired

I can see your tasks are still pending. Any issue?

What I Really Want To Say Out Loud

Stop asking me to do your damn work.

What I'd Say To Avoid Getting Fired

Sorry, but I'm unable to offer any additional support in completing your workload.

What I Really Want To Say Out Loud

Why are you trying to put me down?

What I'd Say To Avoid Getting Fired

Could you please explain what you mean?

What I Really Want To Say Out Loud

Sorry I didn't get back to you for last 3 days. I was too busy doing absolutely nothing on my couch.

What I'd Say To Avoid Getting Fired

My sincere apologies for the delayed response. I really appreciate your patience.

What I Really Want To Say Out Loud

My personal life is none of your business.

What I'd Say To Avoid Getting Fired

Sorry, I prefer not to discuss my personal life at work. Thanks for your understanding.

What I Really Want To Say Out Loud

You're just wasting my time.

What I'd Say To Avoid Getting Fired

In respect of everyone's time, I suggest we meet again once more details become available.

What I Really Want To Say Out Loud

This office is a total circus.

What I'd Say To Avoid Getting Fired

I am afraid there seems to be a lack of coordination in this office.

What I Really Want To Say Out Loud

Staying late for this? Hell no. It's not happening.

What I'd Say To Avoid Getting Fired

As my workday concludes at 5 PM, I'll be able to address this matter in the coming days when my schedule allows.

What I Really Want To Say Out Loud

This meeting is just a literal circle jerk.

What I'd Say To Avoid Getting Fired

I believe we're not making much progress in this meeting.

What I Really Want To Say Out Loud

I told you earlier, but you didn't care to listen.

What I'd Say To Avoid Getting Fired

As per my prediction, this outcome is not surprising to me at all.

What I Really Want To Say Out Loud

Save your personal drama.
No one really cares.

What I'd Say To Avoid Getting Fired

While I understand your
concerns, let's keep our
discussions professional.

What I Really Want To Say Out Loud

Stop f*cking micromanaging me and get the hell off my back before I lose my temper.

What I'd Say To Avoid Getting Fired

I truly appreciate that you're trying to help, but I'm confident in my ability to handle these tasks successfully.

What I Really Want To Say Out Loud

You're painfully slow. Pick up the pace.

What I'd Say To Avoid Getting Fired

We need a faster approach to meet the deadline. Let's speed up.

What I Really Want To Say Out Loud

This isn't my job and I'm not gonna do it.

What I'd Say To Avoid Getting Fired

It seems like this falls more within your duties.

What I Really Want To Say Out Loud

Who screwed up the report again?

What I'd Say To Avoid Getting Fired

I suggest we review the report to identify any errors.

What I Really Want To Say Out Loud

I said what I said.
Deal with it.

What I'd Say To Avoid Getting Fired

I maintain my position on
this matter.

What I Really Want To Say Out Loud

Talk shit? Say it to my face, Motherf*er.

What I'd Say To Avoid Getting Fired

If you have concerns about my work, I'd appreciate discussing them directly.

What I Really Want To Say Out Loud

Are you deliberately ignoring my emails?

What I'd Say To Avoid Getting Fired

Is there someone else I should be contacting regarding this issue? If so then please let me know.

What I Really Want To Say Out Loud

Shut up, you're way too loud.

What I'd Say To Avoid Getting Fired

Please keep things quieter. I need to focus.

What I Really Want To Say Out Loud

F*ck you.

What I'd Say To Avoid Getting Fired

I believe we're done here.

What I Really Want To Say Out Loud

Learn some basic damn manners.

What I'd Say To Avoid Getting Fired

We should maintain a more respectful tone in our conversations.

What I Really Want To Say Out Loud

Who the hell asked for your opinion?

What I'd Say To Avoid Getting Fired

Can you let me know who brought you in on this project?

What I Really Want To Say Out Loud

Stop f*cking disrespecting me

What I'd Say To Avoid Getting Fired

Moving forward, I would appreciate more respect from you to ensure greater mutual benefit.

What I Really Want To Say Out Loud

Seriously, stop singing. I can't tolerate it anymore.

What I'd Say To Avoid Getting Fired

Could you please keep the singing to a minimum in the office? Others may find it difficult to focus.

What I Really Want To Say Out Loud

No more staying late, I've had enough.

What I'd Say To Avoid Getting Fired

I can no longer work late, as it falls outside my responsibilities and hasn't been acknowledged.

What I Really Want To Say Out Loud

Really nobody cares. Get a f*cking life.

What I'd Say To Avoid Getting Fired

I think it's important for both of us to focus more on our own responsibilities and tasks at hand.

What I Really Want To Say Out Loud

Am I speaking to you in a foreign language?

What I'd Say To Avoid Getting Fired

Please feel free to ask if any part of what I've said is not clear.

What I Really Want To Say Out Loud

Oh God, I'm dying here. This job is so boring.

What I'd Say To Avoid Getting Fired

I would really love to gain exposure to different aspects of the business. Would it be possible?

What I Really Want To Say Out Loud

Oh really? Say it again if you have the guts.

What I'd Say To Avoid Getting Fired

I want to make sure I understood correctly. Could you please repeat that?

What I Really Want To Say Out Loud

Stay in your lane, idiot.

What I'd Say To Avoid Getting Fired

I hear you, but I prefer to make decisions about my responsibilities myself.

What I Really Want To Say Out Loud

I have already told you this
a million times.

What I'd Say To Avoid Getting Fired

As I've mentioned a few
times, there are no new
updates yet, but I'll keep
you informed.

What I Really Want To Say Out Loud

I don't do sh*t for free.

What I'd Say To Avoid Getting Fired

These tasks go beyond my current role here. Is there a plan to review this and compensate me accordingly?

What I Really Want To Say Out Loud

Wow, that's officially the dumbest thing you've said this year.

What I'd Say To Avoid Getting Fired

That's an interesting thought, but I think we should reconsider some other options.

What I Really Want To Say Out Loud

Who asked you?

What I'd Say To Avoid Getting Fired

Can you clarify who invited you to join me on this project?

What I Really Want To Say Out Loud

Are you trying to p*ss everyone off?

What I'd Say To Avoid Getting Fired

Let's take a quick break to clear our minds and come back with a fresh perspective.

What I Really Want To Say Out Loud

You are nowhere near my f*cking boss, so how about take a seat?

What I'd Say To Avoid Getting Fired

I appreciate your input, but I am only taking direction from my supervisor on this project. Thanks.

What I Really Want To Say Out Loud

That was a stupid mistake.

What I'd Say To Avoid Getting Fired

I've noticed an error. Let's work together to resolve it.

What I Really Want To Say Out Loud

That's your problem.

What I'd Say To Avoid Getting Fired

That seems like it falls under your job responsibilities.

What I Really Want To Say Out Loud

You are simply a misogynistic a*shole.

What I'd Say To Avoid Getting Fired

We should try to keep our discussions respectful and inclusive of all genders.

What I Really Want To Say Out Loud

I did tell you, didn't I?

What I'd Say To Avoid Getting Fired

I think we have already covered this matte. Am I right?

What I Really Want To Say Out Loud

Oh, look who decided to grace us with their presence.

What I'd Say To Avoid Getting Fired

We are truly honored to have you join us in this meeting.

What I Really Want To Say Out Loud

Are you Serious? That's a terrible f*cking idea.

What I'd Say To Avoid Getting Fired

Do we have full confidence that this is the right solution or are we still exploring alternatives?

What I Really Want To Say Out Loud

That's utter bullsh*t.

What I'd Say To Avoid Getting Fired

It looks highly questionable.

What I Really Want To Say Out Loud

Stop promising unrealistic timelines, deadlines, or other commitments.

What I'd Say To Avoid Getting Fired

Could you please clarify your thinking on these deadlines? I'm having trouble following along.

What I Really Want To Say Out Loud

Your political beliefs are nuts.

What I'd Say To Avoid Getting Fired

Let's prioritize work-related topics and leave politics aside.

What I Really Want To Say Out Loud

I don't give a sh*t; you do it.

What I'd Say To Avoid Getting Fired

I'll rely on your judgment. I'm not particularly passionate one way or the another.

What I Really Want To Say Out Loud

It must be fun to take breaks every 5 minutes like you do.

What I'd Say To Avoid Getting Fired

I'm sure taking breaks so frequently helps with productivity.

What I Really Want To Say Out Loud

If you want it done your way, then do it your fucking self.

What I'd Say To Avoid Getting Fired

I understand that you have a specific vision for this project. So please take the lead and I'll provide all the needed support.

What I Really Want To Say Out Loud

Stop f*cking interrupting me.

What I'd Say To Avoid Getting Fired

I value your feedback, but please let me finish first.

What I Really Want To Say Out Loud

There is absolutely no f*cking reason we should have to have a meeting about this.

What I'd Say To Avoid Getting Fired

Let's keep talking about the project structure over email until we have a meeting agenda.

What I Really Want To Say Out Loud

Proposing to me? No chance in hell.

What I'd Say To Avoid Getting Fired

I like to keep my personal and professional life distinct.

What I Really Want To Say Out Loud

You've really got me twisted.

What I'd Say To Avoid Getting Fired

I think there may have been a miscommunication in my previous email. Let me explain.

What I Really Want To Say Out Loud

Your idea s*cks.

What I'd Say To Avoid Getting Fired

I'm afraid this idea will not work as intended.

What I Really Want To Say Out Loud

Stop f*cking bothering me about this.

What I'd Say To Avoid Getting Fired

Apologies for the delay. Actually, I haven't had any new information, but rest assured, I'll loop you in as soon as I do.

What I Really Want To Say Out Loud

Stop blaming me in public, you coward.

What I'd Say To Avoid Getting Fired

I value your input, but I'd appreciate it if you would keep any future feedback about my work private.

What I Really Want To Say Out Loud

Nice pizza, but it doesn't fix the fact that you pay me like sh*t.

What I'd Say To Avoid Getting Fired

Thanks for the pizza, but it doesn't make up for the fact that many of us are being paid below industry standards.

What I Really Want To Say Out Loud

How the hell can you be this careless?

What I'd Say To Avoid Getting Fired

I suggest double-checking details before finalizing.

What I Really Want To Say Out Loud

I've told you this sh*t 10 damn times.

What I'd Say To Avoid Getting Fired

It seems there may be some confusion, as I have provided this information earlier.

What I Really Want To Say Out Loud

WTF are you even talking about?

What I'd Say To Avoid Getting Fired

Sorry. I'm a bit confused. Can you explain that more in detail?

What I Really Want To Say Out Loud

Standing over me isn't going to speed things up, so just back off.

What I'd Say To Avoid Getting Fired

Thank you for your attention to this matter. I believe I would achieve better results if I work independently.

What I Really Want To Say Out Loud

Quit whining and get to work.

What I'd Say To Avoid Getting Fired

Let's aim to concentrate on solutions rather than the obstacles, so we can stay on track.

What I Really Want To Say Out Loud

I guarantee this project is going to be an absolute flop.

What I'd Say To Avoid Getting Fired

I am not fully on board with this project and I have significant reservations about moving forward.

What I Really Want To Say Out Loud

I'm thrilled to do your work.

What I'd Say To Avoid Getting Fired

Well, I'd be happy to lend a hand today to help meet the deadline, but we should work together to create a more efficient plan for next time.

What I Really Want To Say Out Loud

Google that sh*t yourself.

What I'd Say To Avoid Getting Fired

I'd suggest checking the internet for questions like this. If you still can't find, I'm happy to assist.

What I Really Want To Say Out Loud

Seriously, your constant complaining is s*cking the life out of me.

What I'd Say To Avoid Getting Fired

I understand you have concerns, but it's important to keep our team's spirit up. Let's focus on finding solutions.

What I Really Want To Say Out Loud

This paycheck is a pathetic joke.

What I'd Say To Avoid Getting Fired

I've noticed a discrepancy between my salary and the industry standard for my position. Are there plans to review this in the near future?

What I Really Want To Say Out Loud

Do you ever take responsibility?

What I'd Say To Avoid Getting Fired

It's important to take responsibility when mistakes are made.

What I Really Want To Say Out Loud

If you gave a damn earlier, this wouldn't have happened.

What I'd Say To Avoid Getting Fired

If we had discussed this earlier, I might have found a solution.

What I Really Want To Say Out Loud

I'm done with that client.
End of discussion.

What I'd Say To Avoid Getting Fired

Would it be possible for someone else to handle this client? My previous interactions were not ideal.

What I Really Want To Say Out Loud

Seriously, stop sending me emails every minute.

What I'd Say To Avoid Getting Fired

To ensure effective communication, please combine all daily updates into one email.

What I Really Want To Say Out Loud

Why is everything always about you?

What I'd Say To Avoid Getting Fired

We should focus on the team's needs rather than individual perspectives.

What I Really Want To Say Out Loud

Look, that's not my problem.

What I'd Say To Avoid Getting Fired

I recommend reaching out to someone else for assistance, as it's within their responsibilities.

What I Really Want To Say Out Loud

You're so f*cking clueless.
It's really embarrassing.

What I'd Say To Avoid Getting Fired

I can see there's some
confusion. Let's revisit the
topic to make sure we're
both aligned.

What I Really Want To Say Out Loud

That's not my f*cking job.

What I'd Say To Avoid Getting Fired

At the moment, I am unable to take this on due to my heavy workload, but I would be happy to assist where possible.

What I Really Want To Say Out Loud

You're doing this all wrong, idiot.

What I'd Say To Avoid Getting Fired

I think we should discuss a more effective way to tackle this.

What I Really Want To Say Out Loud

Stop overreacting to every little thing.

What I'd Say To Avoid Getting Fired

I suggest that we focus on finding solutions without unnecessary escalation.

What I Really Want To Say Out Loud

You really didn't bother to read my email, did you?

What I'd Say To Avoid Getting Fired

Let me remind you of what I said in my email. Have you reviewed it yet?

What I Really Want To Say Out Loud

Catch me outside.

What I'd Say To Avoid Getting Fired

I prefer not to discuss personal matters during work hours, but I would be happy to meet after.

What I Really Want To Say Out Loud

You're dumping too much crap on me, stop it.

What I'd Say To Avoid Getting Fired

My current job responsibilities have me at capacity. Could we reassess the workload?

What I Really Want To Say Out Loud

It's all in the damn email, genius. Try reading it.

What I'd Say To Avoid Getting Fired

Please find my initial email, which includes all the details you are looking for.

What I Really Want To Say Out Loud

I'm not a dumbass. I'll crush this in no time.

What I'd Say To Avoid Getting Fired

I assure you I will meet the expectations for this task.

What I Really Want To Say Out Loud

You're not that important.

What I'd Say To Avoid Getting Fired

I think it's essential to view your contributions from a wider perspective.

What I Really Want To Say Out Loud

10 minutes in and you're already changing everything? Seriously?

What I'd Say To Avoid Getting Fired

We've just started and you're already suggesting changes. Could we review the plan before making adjustments?

What I Really Want To Say Out Loud

Figure it out yourself, I'm not your assistant.

What I'd Say To Avoid Getting Fired

My job scope does not allow for additional tasks outside of my assigned duties.

What I Really Want To Say Out Loud

No more goddamn slides!

What I'd Say To Avoid Getting Fired

I think further slides are not required.

What I Really Want To Say Out Loud

Stop throwing me under the bus just to save your own ass.

What I'd Say To Avoid Getting Fired

May I ask that you avoid shifting blame onto me for your own mistakes?

What I Really Want To Say Out Loud

Impressive. You can't do anything right.

What I'd Say To Avoid Getting Fired

We should review our workflow to achieve the best possible outcomes.

What I Really Want To Say Out Loud

You f*cked up big time.

What I'd Say To Avoid Getting Fired

You have given us all an excellent opportunity to learn about this matter.

What I Really Want To Say Out Loud

I didn't give a f*ck about your email.

What I'd Say To Avoid Getting Fired

My apologies for missing your email. I will review it shortly.

What I Really Want To Say Out Loud

Watch your mouth.

What I'd Say To Avoid Getting Fired

It would be great if we could each focus on our own responsibilities rather than discussing my work with others.

What I Really Want To Say Out Loud

How the hell are you still not getting this.

What I'd Say To Avoid Getting Fired

Let me try explaining this in a different way. Which part can I clarify?

What I Really Want To Say Out Loud

Keep messing around and you'll see the consequences.

What I'd Say To Avoid Getting Fired

Do whatever you think is necessary and I'll respond accordingly.

Hello,

Thank you for reading this book. I tried hard to compile 100+ witty alternatives, each designed to help you vent your frustrations while keeping your job. If you truly enjoyed this book and found it useful, please take a moment to **write a review** of it. You can simply scan the following code to leave your review.

Thank you!

Paul Dev

Made in the USA
Monee, IL
20 December 2024

74884476R00059